THE LIBRARY OF INTERIOR DETAIL

COTTAGE

THE LIBRARY OF INTERIOR DETAIL

COTTAGE

*English
Country Style*

ELIZABETH HILLIARD

PHOTOGRAPHS BY JOHN MILLER

BULFINCH PRESS
LITTLE, BROWN AND COMPANY
BOSTON • NEW YORK • TORONTO • LONDON

First North American Edition
First printed in Great Britain in 1994 by Pavilion Books Limited

ISBN 0-8212-2067-5
Library of Congress Catalog Card Number 93-80208

Bulfinch Press is an imprint and trademark of
Little, Brown and Company (Inc.)
Published simultaneously in Canada by
Little, Brown & Company (Canada) Limited

PRINTED IN ITALY

CONTENTS

INTRODUCTION

DETAIL IS THE KEY TO PERFECTION IN ALL THINGS, EVEN DECORATING A COTTAGE. The word 'cottage' means different things to different people, but most would agree that it is a small house, old, in the country, vernacular (built in the local style with local materials), and with a garden. Then what makes it different from a 'house'? Scale, for one thing. Inside, a cottage has small rooms, with ceilings which may be low or relatively high, depending on its age, but are always in proportion to the modest size of the rooms. A cottage also has correspondingly modest aspirations – it has no pretensions to grandeur. It is, or should be, a comfortable, practical and functional living-space.

To many people a cottage represents an ideal state of existence. As soon as you duck under the roses which ramble over the front door and pass into the cool interior, you enter another world. Here life is simple and uncluttered by the nuisances of our ordinary lives: the necessity of earning a living, finding socks that match, and dealing with the tide of unwanted paper that comes through the front door. To live in a cottage is, to the uninitiated, to escape. Even for those people who do actually live in cottages, the ideal burns bright. A friend whose welcoming cottage exudes warmth and overflows with books, pictures and possessions recently confided her own fantasy of living 'in a very simple, graceful way, with one chair, a book, a table, a vase, a picture ... I could only live like that for about half-an-hour! But I like the idea.'

This ideal of simple, rural bliss is far from new. Possibly the most celebrated example is Marie-Antoinette's *Hameau* built in the grounds of the Palace of Versailles at the end of the eighteenth century. This picturesque 'hamlet' consisted of a small mill and a group of cottages, constructed with thatched roofs and distressed walls in the best theatrical scene-painting tradition. Even the woodwork was painted with cracks to create a convincing impression of age and weathering. The story goes that the fated French queen would dress in her own picturesque version of a milkmaid's garments and imagine herself an innocent rustic, released from the burden of cares and responsibilities laid upon her by an unforgiving world. Certainly she found refuge there from the stultifying formality and political intrigue of the court, whatever clothes she actually wore, and whether or not she ever milked a cow.

In England, the romantic cottage tradition was pursued equally enthusiastically, though perhaps with less extravagance. Queen Charlotte's Cottage in the grounds of what is now the Royal Botanic Gardens at Kew in London, was built in 1772. A popular summerhouse and private picnic place for the family of King George III, the cottage was sited in woodland carpeted with bluebells. The roof was thatched and the interior was decorated with paintings of cottage flowers in a scheme designed, and possibly executed, by the Princess Elizabeth, George III and Queen Charlotte's third daughter.

Queen Charlotte's Cottage is an example of the picturesque cult which caught the imagination of late eighteenth-century and early nineteenth-century English landowners, and which resulted in the construction of many a *cottage orné*. These self-consciously rustic buildings were constructed as lodges to great houses, punctuating the carefully engineered landscapes of such designers as Humphry Repton, and were also incorporated in housing schemes for farm labourers. Well-built and commodious by most contemporary cottage standards, *cottages ornés* were often lived in by genuine working people. In contrast, many much larger 'cottages' were built around the same time for the gentry and the newly rich who liked the look of them and were inspired by the idea of cottage life. Even today, some houses with the word 'cottage' in their names look more like mansions.

Generally, however, the word 'cottage' is used to describe a pretty, small-scale house, usually in the country but possibly also in a town or city; often detached from other buildings but not necessarily so. Estate agents frequently use the word, seemingly with the intention of conveying not only some idea of the property's size and scale but also implying that it possesses a certain air of solidity and quiet gentility; it is not an ex-council house, nor does it quite qualify as a grander 'residence'.

Ann Allison worked this sampler in 1797 at the age of seventeen. Samplers often include mottoes and quotations dealing with death and God, and this one is no exception. 'How frail is human life', it gasps, 'how short the span how fleetin (sic) is (sic) days of mortal man each moment as it flies cuts short our breath and whispers in our ears prepare for death.'

The gentility implied by the description of a building as a cottage is a fairly recent notion. For centuries, the reality of life for many cottage dwellers was uncomfortable poverty. There was no sanitation, water had to be carried in, furniture was restricted to a few items, and, in the hours of darkness, heat and light were largely limited to whatever the fire or range could provide. In such a context the concept of interior decoration obviously did not exist. Life was grindingly hard work and death more likely to be the result of disease or childbirth rather than old age.

Fortunately for us, this depressing piece of history is just that – a thing of the past. Today there is hardly a cottage without central heating and a washing machine, let alone one without an indoor lavatory. In the type of cottages with which this book is concerned, any cooking apparatus that needs feeding with solid fuel is likely to be an Aga. In many cases, such traditional cookers have been superseded by halogen rings and the microwave. Decorating a cottage interior is not simply a practical necessity but provides a positive opportunity to create a home that is an expression of who you are and what kind of life you lead.

In the simplest cottage, such as a Scottish 'wee butt 'n' ben', there might be two rooms, with the front door opening directly into the first. This was originally the everyday room, used for cooking, eating, living and sleeping. Such use of the kitchen (apart from the sleeping) still prevails today. In larger houses the kitchen might once have been the domain of a servant or staff – not so in a cottage, then or now. The person doing the cooking is probably also the one who is minding the children and trying to finish the ironing in time to welcome the visitors who will sit at the kitchen table for the meal being prepared.

There is rarely space in a cottage for a whole room to be devoted to the function of a dining room – even were it wanted. A straw poll today reveals that many people, especially of the younger generations, prefer to entertain in the kitchen so that they are not excluded from the fun when serving and clearing. The kitchen is likewise a room for leisure activities such as reading the newspaper, writing letters, watching television or just sitting and talking with a glass of wine at six o'clock.

A recessed panel for a doormat, original to this Victorian cottage, takes a size of mat that is still available today. The edging is made from beaten copper, the door is painted with an off-the-shelf colour, and the fossil on the doorstep is an heirloom.

Entertaining in the kitchen epitomizes just one aspect of the informality of cottage life. A cottage is the sort of home which, far from intimidating approaching friends, invites them to open the door and walk in, after ringing the bell or knocking as a matter of courtesy. The door may be left ajar, or even wide open, in fine weather. Many cottage front doors open directly into the sitting room or kitchen – an arrangement which demands a certain agility in immediately removing muddy and wet clothes in bad weather, probably in a small space. The advantage of this layout, however, is the luxury of having warm, scented air and the sound of buzzing bees wafting directly into the sitting room or kitchen in summer.

The different types of people who are attracted to cottages vary today more than ever before. Social background no longer limits the type of building which others think it appropriate we should inhabit. Everyone can appreciate not only the charm and compact good looks which a cottage home offers, but also its practicality. Thick walls help to retain heat and resist extremes of weather. Small windows lose less heat than large ones, even if a cottage with larger windows is lighter; small windows also need less curtain fabric to keep out light and cold – that's if there are no shutters. Modestly sized rooms are quicker and cheaper to heat, especially if they also have low ceilings; they are also easier to keep clean and need less furniture. Several small rooms have an advantage over fewer large ones in that they can be dedicated to different people and purposes – a great advantage in a large or busy family. And if you leave something in your bedroom, or are tidying up after other people, you don't have to walk miles to complete the task.

Although a cottage should have no pretentions to grandeur, that does not mean to say that to be in keeping with the building's history its contents should necessarily be rough-hewn and spartan. This may have been true of poor labourers' dwellings, but some buildings that would qualify as cottages were lived in by the genteel poor: spinster aunts, gentlemen of modest means, or retired people such as rectors, housekeepers and governesses. Items of unfashionable furniture would sometimes be passed down from the big house when new were bought, to such needy people as these. An example of similar demotion comes from a grand country house, where an auctioneer discovered a complete set of Chippendale dining chairs furnishing the servants' attics – sent there in the nineteenth century when a new set (now considered less beautiful and valuable) arrived. Fine furniture of any period, along with fine pictures and objects, can look at home in a cottage, so long as their scale is compatible with the building itself.

A leg of this comfortable upholstered chair simply fell off one day, so the owner propped up the corner with a pile of paperbacks. In a lived-in cottage, such charming temporary measures tend to become permanent ... The chair was upholstered in the 1970s using an Osborne and Little fabric; it may be a little grubby now, but otherwise it looks as fresh today as it did then.

Another common and invaluable source of furniture is the family. There can hardly be a cottage which is not partly furnished with cast-offs and inherited pieces, often upholstered furniture such as sofas and armchairs. And no English interior, be it a cottage or a castle, is complete without the embrace of a comfortable armchair in which to curl up by the fire at the end of a busy day. A pile of small cushions, embroidered by forebears or made up from scraps of velvet, silk and ethnic fabrics, is likely to be near at hand to guarantee your comfort. Even the tiniest cottage can accommodate a small sofa, since the English love affair with this piece of furniture results in it being made in every imaginable size, shape and style. Bedrooms often contain small upholstered chairs which were once nursery nursing chairs or 'boudoir' chairs. And often one kitchen chair, if not actually upholstered, will be made comfortable with several squashy cushions.

Keeping true both to the building and to yourself is the key to decorating a cottage. Just as no one but an extreme purist would suggest that we do without the conveniences of modern plumbing, heating, lighting or household machinery, so it would be equally absurd to insist on doing without modern materials, patterns, colours, carpets, interior sprung beds and other comforts of modern decorating and furnishing. The answer is to find a middle path, and the first step towards finding the way is gradually to educate your eye, not just in the broader view, but in the details of true cottage style. You can do this by visiting authentic old properties which are open to the public, by reading relevant books and magazines, and by developing a critical sense of what is wrong with cottages that are inappropriately decorated.

It is instructive, if a little depressing, to catalogue the horrors that are sometimes perpetrated on cottages. Fakes are the most obvious – fake wooden beams on walls and ceilings; fake stonework round fireplaces. A building should be allowed to be itself, and should never be dressed up in unconvincing tat. Varnish is often another horror, whether it appears as glossy gunge on woodwork, stonework or flag floors, or on dark stained wooden replacement windows that should be painted. Structural materials should either be left in their natural state, or plastered over where appropriate. If you visit cottages with exposed beams in the walls, you will often see that the wood has been hacked into in many places with small strokes of the hammer and chisel. This shows that the beam was once plastered over, the hacking providing a key for the plaster to grip.

Too much fuss and frills should be avoided, especially around windows; simple curtain dressing is preferable and, in many cases, shutters are better still. Too much fitted furniture can kill the interior of a cottage. Fitted bookcases and the occasional wardrobe may be suitable – they do, after all, give the maximum storage space in oddly shaped corners – but Dallas-style bedrooms are not. Garish or dreary modern colour and pattern – in pattered carpets on the floors, the fabric of upholstery and curtains, and lurid colours on painted and papered walls and tiles – is another true horror perpetrated on old cottages.

It is sad, too, to see internal doors which have been replaced at some point in the twentieth century by hollow flush doors with gaudy elaborate handles instead of knobs or latches. Doors can be replaced fairly easily, but if your doors are flush it is worth investigating to see if they

This door was recently stripped and then fed with a half-and-half mixture of linseed oil and turpentine. The turps encourages the oil to go on smoothly and sink into the wood. The rim latch is a particularly pretty example.

have panels which have simply been covered over with a piece of hardboard. If this is the case, the door within would be of solid timber so it should be heavy and fairly dull to the knock. Replacement doors should ideally be old ones. These can often be found in local auctions and sales, in reclamation yards, and by advertising in the local paper, but be aware of the size of your door openings. There was probably no such thing as a

Wood, plaster and clay tile ... the timeless honesty of these fine materials shines through countless scabby layers of old paint and the dirt of ages. This cottage has escaped modernization and tampering in all but the most essential ways, and consequently retains an exceptionally unspoilt appearance and atmosphere.

'standard' size when your cottage was built, and sizes vary wildly. In the end it may be necessary to have doors custom-made, or modern solid timber doors (now available in some quite acceptable designs from DIY superstores) especially made to fit.

Metal Norfolk or Suffolk latches can be bought in any good ironmonger, and specialist suppliers of ironwork also offer some interesting designs. Brass, iron, wooden and china doorknobs can be bought new, or, even better, collected in junk shops and jumble sales. Local auctions are another possible source; if the lot includes a jumble of other architectural ironmongery, you will have to buy it all together – but you may find all kinds of old things for your home in the box or bag. Warehouses dealing in stripped pine may sell off the door furniture and other ironmongery separately. Rim latches, which sit on the surface of the door, are an attractive alternative to mortice ones, which must be embedded in the thickness of the door. The design of these has not changed in generations, and can be seen in any good ironmonger. They can also be hunted down in the same way as knobs and will sometimes be found with the original knobs still attached.

Floors can either make a room beautiful, or be an eyesore. If your boards are sound, simply feed them with linseed, stale olive or Danish oil and polish them with wax. Too much carpet, covering all floors to the edge and deadening contact with stone and wood on the ground floor, is unnecessary. Rugs, or a piece of carpet bound around the edges (any good carpet shop should do this for you), generally look better, and can easily be changed or taken with you if you move. Fitted carpet does however feel less inappropriate in a bedroom than in most other rooms, and is useful where the existing boards are not in good enough condition to leave bare, even around the edge of a room. Grass matting is more sympathetic than carpet to the age and style of old cottages and is now widely available in a range of colours and patterned weaves.

Poor boards can, however, usually be repaired and painted. If you can't obtain floor paint in a suitably subtle colour it is possible to make an emulsion-painted floor fairly hardwearing by the addition of many layers of matt or satin floor varnish. And real linoleum (as opposed to vinyl) which is made in a kaleidoscope of rich colours, makes a practical floorcovering in a kitchen, scullery/laundry, bathroom or any other 'messy' room. Flagstones can often be rescued, with work, from layers of asphalt and concrete. If they are beyond saving, tiles of many types and even concrete slabs can successfully replace them. These can be laid in a dark-and-light chequerboard pattern and polished with wax to make a sympathetic floor, hardwearing and with a lively but suitably authentic appearance.

The cottages photographed for this book have been decorated with enthusiasm and imagination by their owners. The materials used are not always old-fashioned but have been chosen for their empathy with the buildings. Some traditional materials, such as distemper and old-style emulsion paints, have recently become more readily available as a result of renewed interest in old buildings and authentic decorative materials and techniques. The National Trust range of paints is manufactured in England by the only company still in full-scale production of distemper. The paint is made with casein (an environmentally-friendly binder derived from whey of milk) as opposed to the commonly used acrylic binders, resulting in a gloriously soft, chalky finish. Some of their subtle, glowing colours can be seen in the photographs here.

The colours used in these cottages vary hugely, from white and delicate stripes to rich, strong ochre, red, green and blue, but they are never brilliant. Floors are polished, tiled or painted, covered with rush matting, old kelims and rugs, but are never concealed beneath wall-to-wall carpeting. Kitchens are rarely fitted, unless you count the sink unit. Furniture comes from all periods, as do pictures and china, and the periods all combine successfully because everything has been chosen with love and care by people for whom no detail is too small. For the same reason, valuable antiques happily coexist with jumble sale bargains and high street purchases.

Wherever there is practical space in these houses, you will find treasures on display. Many cottages have thick walls which result in deep windowsills – ideal for display, except where there are shutters. Plates can be hung on walls and china and objects arranged along the tops of cupboards, in bookshelves, or on mantelshelves. Pictures will always look better if arranged as a scheme for the whole room, rather than being dotted about at random. If you have only a few, small pictures, hang one above another, or several in a group. If they share a characteristic, such as subject matter or colour range, or if they are painted or drawn in the same medium, the group will be all the more interesting.

The statement 'books do furnish a room', made famous by the novelist Anthony Powell, is undoubtedly true. Books can also take a room over with alarming speed unless they are well organized, but no home ever feels complete without them. An alcove or recess, an entire wall or even a whole room can be lined with bookshelves, with the furniture placed in front. As well as being attractive, books provide some insulation against sound, a bonus if your cottage has partition walls which are barely more than boards.

Lighting in a cottage, as in any house, needs to be practical as well as visually pleasing. Pendant lightbulbs in the middle of ceilings are rarely attractive, and in a cottage with low ceilings they can be dangerously impractical. Many people deplore modern spotlights and downlighters, including the author Hugh Lander, whose books on cottages are a rich source of information and delight. In certain circumstances, however, they are a practical option, and if cleverly placed they may be aesthetically innocuous.

Sunlight casts a dramatic shadow through the back of this Windsor chair on to the plain white-painted plaster behind. Dark wood against white walls provides a clean, bold contrast which sums up the fresh simplicity of English cottage style.

An alternative is to use wall brackets, but these too can be unsatisfactory, both in appearance and when they interfere with furniture, bookshelving or picture arrangements. Lamps on tables are almost always the best solution in cottages, but to be totally practical at least one in each room should be wired to switch on at the door – a requirement which can cause difficulties. It is best to take each room individually and work out a tailor-made solution to the problem of lighting.

The fireplace is a vital source of visual comfort in English cottages in winter, as well as a source of heat. A crackling fire is ideal, whether in a grate or a stove, but sometimes it is preferable or necessary to have a gas fire. This could be a real-effect fire (now so convincing it is difficult to tell the difference at a glance) although these do not provide heat as efficiently as the real thing. A gas-fired stove will give a roaring heat and look convincing too.

Central heating is another modern convenience which needs careful thought. If radiators are already in position and there is no question of changing them, paint them the same colour as the walls for minimum intrusion. It might be possible to change some of your slightly antiquated 'modern' radiators for new ones which may be a fraction of the size but equally (or more) thermally efficient. If you are installing a completely new system, consider choosing cast-iron radiators, which take longer to become hot but retain the heat for longer. These are available in some traditional designs, and in simple modern designs which can look appropriate in old buildings.

If you treat your cottage home as a friend it will surely repay the compliment. Consider in detail its character, and enjoy it, don't fight it. Dress it considerately, not only to reflect your personality and lifestyle, your taste and preferences, but also bearing in mind the age of your home, its natural form and features. Make the most of what it is, rather than trying to make it look like something it is not. Each of the interiors of the cottages shown here is practical and, above all, personal. Each has been built up gradually, sympathetically, on a budget and without the help of interior designers. Their inhabitants have decorated them in such a way that they are irresistibly inviting. The country cottages shown in this book have been chosen to provide you with inspiration and a rich source of new ideas. We hope that after reading this book you will find that you are seeing with new eyes, and that no cottage will ever look quite the same again.

DOORS & WINDOWS

DOORS AND WINDOWS ARE THE EYES, EARS AND LUNGS OF A HOUSE. THE WAY THEY LOOK AND FEEL — THEIR STYLE AND THE MATERIALS FROM WHICH THEY ARE MADE, THEIR PAINTED OR POLISHED FINISHES, THEIR KNOBS AND CATCHES — IS VITAL TO THE APPEARANCE OF A COTTAGE HOME.

Old rim latches, which sit on the surface of the door rather than being fitted into its thickness, can be picked up in junk shops and markets. When cleaned, painted and oiled inside, they should give good service. New rim latches are still available from ironmongers.

This pitch pine door, complete with stock lock with pierced iron mounts, was found being used to restrain hay in a barn. The current owners, who were renovating their cottage at the time, rescued it and had a doorway specially altered to fit. The keys are old but do not match the lock.

An idiosyncratic cat-door. A round hole was cut in the wood and the portcullis-style door added on the inside, with a bolt to keep it open when the family, and cat, are in residence.

*This old plank door was installed in the 1970s to separate the kitchen from
the larder beyond. The larder also has a door, which leads into the garden,
so the iron loop below the Suffolk latch is intended to secure the kitchen
against unwanted intruders.*

A narrow ledge above a doorway is a good place on which to display small objects and pictures. The wool picture is the work of a sailor and is part of a collection, one of which incorporates the sailor's hatband showing the name of his ship. The bottles are salt glazed and would have been used to hold inks or dyes.

An old wrought iron casement window latch with a curly tail makes a charming change from most bland modern window furniture.

Bare Camel-stone mullions frame leaded lights in this east-facing window. The leadwork was replaced ten years ago by a local craftsman, found through the local business telephone directory. The glass bottles were dug up in the garden.

Roses arranged in a Victorian china boot on a sunny white-painted windowsill. A few leaves of ivy can be seen through the window. In the garden below, copper leafed cherry trees stand out against the delicate foliage of silver poplars, with lush English countryside stretching into the distance.

HALLS, STAIRS & FLOORS

FLAGSTONES, POLISHED OR PAINTED
BOARDS, RUGGED POTTERY TILES, EXOTIC
RUGS ON RUSH MATTING, THE SCARRED
TREADS OF AN OLD STAIRCASE . . . THE
FEEL AND LOOK OF WHAT IS UNDERFOOT
MAKES ALL THE DIFFERENCE TO A HOME.
COTTAGE HALLS, FLOORS AND STAIRS ARE
UNPRETENTIOUS AND SIMPLY FURNISHED.

*These stairs lead from the ground to the first floor. A
flight from the first to second floors is oak, but this lower
flight was apparently replaced in the nineteenth century
with these lightweight treads and risers. The tongue and
groove dado was probably added at the same time.*

Coats, hats, gloves, scarves, boots, a
basket, umbrellas and miscellaneous
sporting equipment jostle for position
in a typical cottage hallway which
doubles as a cloakroom. No English
country hall is complete without an
umbrella stand to receive umbrellas
still dripping with rain, and a
flagstone floor is likewise ideal for a
hall in this damp climate.

The ideal cottage has a garden. This seventeenth- century flagstone hall floor is the natural indoor resting place for gardening clutter, including early-twentieth-century galvanized watering cans and a pair of workmen's clogs from Brittany. The owner claims that these are ideal gardening footwear in the damp English climate, keeping one's feet both dry and comfortable.

The stairs in this Victorian cottage rise straight up between two walls, from just inside the front door, to a tiny landing at the top. The wall, skirting and stairs have all been painted with paints from the National Trust range, based on colours in historic houses: emulsion has been used on the wall, with dead flat (matt) oil applied to skirting, treads and risers.

This beautiful oak staircase looks entirely at home in a seventeenth-century cottage in Suffolk, even though it is actually a modern adaptation. The bare wood has not been covered with unnecessary carpet.

The threshold of a room showing old, stained and dirty boards on one side, and similar boards which have been painted on the other. Emulsion-painted boards have been sealed and made fairly hardwearing by applying layer upon layer of satin varnish, but special floor paints could also be used.

An original floor such as this is a treasure beyond compare which cannot be reproduced today. The sheen on its surface is the result of centuries of polishing and use and its dusky colour is caused by the natural darkening of oak exposed to sunlight. The boards are made from seasoned oak and each is 30 cm (12 in) wide.

Yorkshire flagstones have been cut into squares and set diagonally within a rectangular frame to create this pretty hall floor.

The flagstone floor of this kitchen is original to the cottage, built in 1877. The owners removed layers of vinyl flooring, asphalt and concrete to reveal the flags beneath. They are untreated, their patina being the result of much use by adults and small children. Occasionally they are scrubbed. The chair was found in a mill sale.

PAINT

COLOURS IN THE ENGLISH COTTAGE VARY
GREATLY, FROM WHITE TO THE RICH
TONES OF OCHRE, RED, GREEN AND BLUE
WHICH INTRODUCE WARMTH AND LIFE ON
RAINY DAYS AND GLOW IN THE SUMMER
SUNSHINE. TYPES OF PAINT INCLUDE
ORIGINAL WHITEWASH, MODERN ACRYLICS
AND OLD-FASHIONED DISTEMPER, IN
FASHION AGAIN.

*Pitted layers of tinted whitewash and plaster have
taken on an abstract, almost sculptural, quality. Each
colour was mixed individually, the blue shades being
made with a powder known in Yorkshire as 'dolly blue'
which was added to laundry to make it blue-white.*

41

A wonderfully distressed, painted wooden plank door with sneck-latch (the sneck is the curved lever which lifts the latch), reveals centuries of decorative attention and wear. A similarly dramatic effect could be achieved by an enthusiastic amateur or a specialist decorator.

The upstairs of this cottage is now a home for doves, one of whom favours a wall-mounted, rush-seated chair as a comfortable place to sit. Layers of paint on the walls have crumbled to reveal the many different colours applied over generations.

Emulsion (on walls) and dead flat (matt) oil paints from the National Trust range – here Berrington Blue and Book Room Red. Both shades are well-suited to this Victorian cottage. The blue is a copy of a mid-nineteenth-century colour found in the boudoir at Berrington Hall in Hereford and Worcester; the red is also mid-nineteenth-century and is derived from paint found at Attingham Park in Shropshire.

A comfortable wooden chair casts a shadow on an original studwork partition wall in a seventeenth-century Somerset cottage. When artists James and Kate Lynch bought the house this wall was whitewashed; James toned down the modern paints with varnish mixed with small quantities of burnt umber, yellow ochre and black artist's oil paint.

The plaster between the external studwork on the lower part of this wall is new and unpainted. It was applied as usual and then brushed to look rough and old.

A collection of Victorian jelly moulds, glass bottles dug up in the garden and a
bulbous fly catcher gleam against a painted wall. The rich green is a mixture of
standard off-the-shelf colours. The collection of glassware is arranged on oak
shelves, formerly used as a pan rack, screwed to the wall.

A soft, strong red provides a rich background for these four pictures, mounted in wood and gilt frames. Each has a family connection, having been drawn, stitched or painted by the owner's forebears. They are more visually interesting grouped in this way than they would be if dotted around the walls of the room.

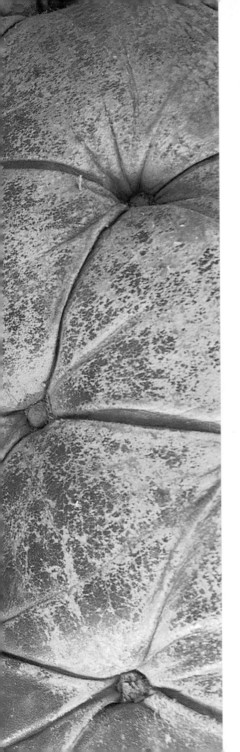

PATTERN

BEAMED CEILINGS CREATE A PATTERN IN
THEMSELVES, WHICH CHANGES TO A
THREE-DIMENSIONAL PUZZLE WHEN THE
CEILING IS OPENED TO THE EVES.
ELSEWHERE, PRINTED AND WOVEN
FABRICS, PATCHWORK, CROCHET AND
CROSS-STITCH BRING APPLIED PATTERN
INTO THE COTTAGE INTERIOR.

*Cushions covered with pieces of kelim are piled up on a
battered leather-covered chesterfield. The sofa's
upholstery buttons make a geometric pattern of their
own, while the soft brown of the leather provides the
delicious vegetable-dye colours of the cushions with a
harmonious background.*

The brilliantly-coloured crocheted shawl which livens up this dull sofa is an heirloom, made by the owner's great-grandmother. She made a different shawl for each of her three grandchildren and seven great-grandchildren. What looks like oak panelling behind the sofa is actually an original elm studwork partition. The other side of this wall is shown in the upper illustration on page 45.

*This cushion looks as if it is generations old but was actually made by the house owner's mother-in-law. The chair
is a particularly pretty example of a nineteenth-century spindleback.*

After decades of use, the colours are fading and the weave of this linen union is showing through the printed pattern. This is a detail of the loose cover on an upholstered armchair. Floral patterned fabric has been an essential element in many a typical English interior, at least since the Victorian mania for flowers.

The elaborate geometric pattern and brilliant colours of this kelim enliven a cottage sitting room. Originating from the Van area of south eastern Anatolia, the rug is around sixty years old and is laid on Indian hemp matting. This in turn covers a floor of which part is concrete and part wooden boards.

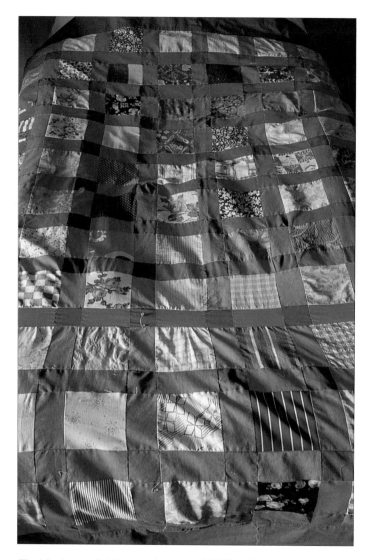

The rich colours and rigid geometric pattern of this Victorian patchwork quilt make a strong impact in this dark, low-ceilinged bedroom.

The red-and-white striped cover on this painted iron bedstead is dramatic and modern-looking. It is actually Victorian, bought in County Durham in the north of England, and is extremely warm, consisting of two layers, one cotton and one woollen. Each stripe is a separate piece of cotton sewn to the next.

Pattern need not be applied – here the structural members of a magnificent beamed roof make a three-dimensional geometric design. The spaces between have been plastered up to the eaves and painted ochre, a strong colour that tones well with the golden brown of the wood.

FURNITURE

ALL TYPES OF FURNITURE LOOK AT HOME
IN A COTTAGE — FROM THE RUGGED AND
WORN RUSTIC CHAIR TO A HUGE BOOK-
CASE, MADE SPECIALLY TO FIT THE SPACE.
UPHOLSTERED CHAIRS AND SOFAS ARE
COSY AND WELCOMING; CUPBOARDS ARE
INVALUABLE. APPARENTLY GRAND FURNI-
TURE MAY NOT BE ALL IT SEEMS.

*This Windsor chair was once stained black but the stain
has worn away in the places where the chair has had most
use – on the seat and on the arms – allowing the golden
colour and pretty grain of the beech to show through.*

Above. *This imposing oak dresser is actually a 'marriage' of bits and pieces of furniture. The 1701 date plate is detachable. Dark, glossily polished wood makes a magnificent background for this collection of china which includes pieces by Wedgwood, Ashworth, Rockingham and Spode, as well as by the contemporary potter Juliet Beaumont.*
A mug made by her hangs on a brass cup hook decorated with a face (right).

Above. *An old painted cupboard,
rescued from the potting shed of a
friend who was moving house,
makes a magical still life, piled up
with terracotta flower pots.*
Left. *Three separate pieces of
furniture, none of them grand, are
piled on top of each other to
magnificent effect in this high-
ceilinged Victorian cottage. The
small chest of drawers on top holds
treasures; the big chest of drawers
was found in the house, hidden
behind fitted furniture.*

The arm of a wonderfully worn leather-covered chesterfield sofa, showing the elaborate detailing of the ruched and piped upholstery.

One corner of this sitting room is dominated by a bookcase and armchair (see also page 13). The bookcase was made especially for the space by a local joiner and painted to match the walls. The floor is also painted, and the rug was bought from a village sale for a few pounds.

A small Victorian iron and brass double bed, just 1.35m (4 ft 6 in) wide and draped in white, is in keeping with the scale and simplicity of this airy cottage. The bed was found in a London auction. The wallpaper is a delicate pink-and-white stripe from Laura Ashley.

THE
FIREPLACE

A ROARING FIRE OR GLOWING STOVE IS THE FOCUS OF A ROOM, ESPECIALLY DURING THE COLD WET MONTHS OF AN ENGLISH WINTER. THE HEART REJOICES IN TEA, OR A HOT TODDY, TAKEN SITTING BY THE FIRE. THE MANTELPIECE, MEAN-WHILE, IS A USEFUL PLACE FOR MISCELLANEOUS POSSESSIONS AND POSTCARDS.

Fire dogs are free-standing supports for logs in a large open hearth known as a down hearth. This one has a curly heart-shaped end.

This type of wide open fireplace, known as a down hearth, is most people's ideal of a cottage fireside. Warm and welcoming, it also provides the room with a visual focus. The fire is built on free-standing fire dogs, but it could equally well be made in a fire basket in this sort of hearth. The mantelshelf inevitably collects miscellaneous clutter. The room's furniture and decorations are refreshingly austere.

This stove is a gas-powered modern version of a Victorian design, and is not too big in appearance for the scale of the room while giving out plenty of heat. The pot is round-bottomed and African, with an imprinted pattern. The dried roses and cache-pot were found in a village sale. The hearth is covered with black quarry tiles.

Above. *A wonderful jumble of possessions on a mantelshelf, including old matchboxes, clay pipes, a doll, pottery and a candlestick.*
Right. *This carved overmantel is another 'marriage' (see dresser on page 58), this time of a Victorian centre panel and two older grotesque figures. The cups and saucers commemorate royal events, the jug and candlesticks are English and the shells were found in Africa.*

KITCHENS
&
BATHROOMS

THE COTTAGE KITCHEN IS A WARM,
FRIENDLY PLACE, WHERE AN OLD DRESSER
RUBS SHOULDERS WITH AN AGA OR SECOND-
HAND GAS COOKER. IT IS RARELY FITTED
OUT IN THE LATEST TECHNOLOGY; RATHER,
IT EXUDES OLD-FASHIONED CHARM, WHILE
DISPLAYING GARLIC, OLIVE OIL AND SPICES
ON ITS SHELVES.

These storage cupboards are original to the cottage.
They support a row of mugs including some Cornish
Kitchenware and some Spode Blue Italian. Tea towels
and tablecloth (all second-hand or high-street
purchases) dry on a creel suspended from the ceiling.

A mass of kitchen china, collected over thirty-five years, crowds this primitive dresser.
Some pieces have been brought from France and Italy, but most are English. Nothing
matches, and the collection is designed for use (breakages are regrettable but not
mourned) rather than display. Patches of the clay lump walls can be seen behind.

Miscellaneous picturesque kitchen utensils hanging from cup hooks under a fishy collection. They include a rabbit chocolate mould, egg slicer, mincer and barbecue tongs. The green enamel object was an iron stand, for placing the iron on when you took it off the fire. If you filled it with coals it could also help keep the iron hot.

Blue and white china has an enduring charm, and none more so than this classic striped design known as Cornish Kitchenware. It is still made in Derbyshire, where it originated in the early twentieth century, by the company T. G. Green of Church Gresley.

Most of the cottages in this book have unfitted kitchens. Here, a second-hand gas cooker stands next to the bottom half of a 1930s pre-utility dresser with useful enamel worktop. Ingredients like olive oil have now joined Marmite as staples of English food.

Above. *This magnificent cottage range is no longer used for cooking, but it keeps the kitchen warm and is a useful incinerator for disposable nappies. The design was mass produced in the second half of the nineteenth century and was especially popular in the north of England.*

*A cottage breakfast table, with tea, brown bread and home-made jam in the
kitchen of woven-textile designer Georgina Cardew. The table was painted and
decorated with emulsion and then varnished.*

An elderly porcelain sink with integral draining board is still in use, with updated plumbing. Rubber tap spouts are invaluable and cost little from ironmongers and village stores. This cottage is on a hill, so the ground drops away steeply from the front door while the kitchen at the back is below ground level.

This bath and basin with their handsome taps were in the cottage when it was bought in the eighties. Old taps and bathroom china usually cost a fraction of the price of new, and can be tracked down in markets and through advertisements in local papers, parish magazines and post office windows.

Light reflects off white-painted tongue-and-groove partitioning and a panelled door opening on to cellar steps. Gloss paint can help reflect light into darkish corners of cottage kitchens, as can mirrors hung on walls, and solid door panels replaced with glass.

Shells collected on summer holidays in Scotland have here been piled up on the sill of a bathroom window, in front of a seaside painting made by a friend. The modern net curtain gives a fresh and airy feel to the composition.

ACKNOWLEDGEMENTS

DEDICATION

For Jan and Georgina

Elizabeth Hilliard is grateful to many people whose kindness and enthusiasm have helped her with this book, but she especially thanks the following: Emma Armitage; Kate Bell; Felicity Bryan; Georgina Cardew and Philip Austen; Paul Burcher; Katrin Cargill; Christopher Corr; Mr and Mrs Paul Farmiloe; T. G. Green (producers of blue and white Cornish Kitchenware, Clover-leaf Group Ltd, Church Gresley, Swadlincote, Derbyshire DE11 8EF, telephone 0283 217 981); Tom Helme; Karen Hill; Mrs David Hilliard; Historic Royal Palaces; Karen Humphries and Simon Rose; Alan James; Rachel King; Hugh Lander; James and Kate Lynch; Tessa Mackay; Barbara Mellor and Gavin Harding; National Trust Paints (available from Farrow and Ball, Uddens Trading Estate, Wimborne, Dorset BH21 7NL, telephone 0202 876 141); Christina Probert Jones; William Selka; Lucy Stewart-Roberts and Christopher Hollis; Sarah Riddick; Helen Sudell; Susan Taylor; Mr and Mrs Nicholas Walker; Deborah Walter; Maryanne Wilkins.

Above all, she thanks John Miller whose beautiful photographs make this book what it is.